COPING
WITH
GRIEF

PASTOR STEPHEN RATHOD

Scripture quotations marked AMP are taken from the Amplified® Bible (AMP), Copyright © 2015 by The Lockman Foundation. Used by permission. www.Lockman.org.

Scripture quotations marked AMPC are taken from the Amplified, Classic Edition ®. Copyright © 1954, 1958, 1962, 1964, 1965, 1987 by The Lockman Foundation. Used by permission.

Scripture quotations marked CEB are taken from the Common English Bible. Copyright © 2011 by Common English Bible. Public Domain.

Scripture quotations marked NLT are taken from the Holy Bible, New Living Translation, Copyright © 1996, 2004, 2015 by Tyndale House Foundation. Used by permission of Tyndale House Publishers, Inc., Carol Stream, Illinois 60188. All rights reserved.

Scripture quotations marked NKJV are taken from the New King James Version®. Copyright © 1982 by Thomas Nelson. Used by permission. All rights reserved.

Scripture quotations marked KJV are taken from the King James Version of the Bible. Public domain.

Coping with Grief
Copyright © 2021 by Pastor Stephen Rathod
ISBN: 978-1-949106-68-8

Published by Word and Spirit Publishing
P.O. Box 701403
Tulsa, Oklahoma 74170
wordandspiritpublishing.com

Printed in the United States of America. All rights reserved under International Copyright Law. Content and/or cover may not be reproduced in whole or in part in any form without the expressed written consent of the Publisher.

CONTENTS

Introduction v

Chapter 1: What Is Grief? 1

Chapter 2: The Stages of Grief 7

Chapter 3: Practically Processing
                Grief 13

Chapter 4: Be Prepared! 31

Chapter 5: We Do Not Grieve
                as the World Grieves 37

Chapter 6: You Are Not Alone 45

Introduction

This message has been in my heart for a long time. As the church, the body of Christ as a whole, we've taught so many things. We have taught on victory, on hope, and on faith. When we minister on such things, then people get happy, shout, and run up and down the aisles. Truth is truth—and these things must still be taught in the church today, but not at the expense of other things.

There is one such thing, an emotion that is cold and crippling but which all who walk this earth must learn how to navigate through. Yet we, the church as a whole, have failed to address it. This gap in our armor I am referring to is ***grief***.

We preach victory, at the same time treating people who are in the midst of pain and suffering from loss as if it's their own fault. We've been guilty of shooting our wounded instead of helping them.

No longer.

If you are in the midst of grief, you are not the only one, and you do

Introduction

not have to traverse the bumpy road ahead alone.

There is a road ahead of all of us concerning grief. Grief is not something we can avoid in this life. It is simply a matter of time. Everything in this world has a beginning and an end. Loss and grief are just as much a part of life as anything else. This is why it is so essential that we learn how to navigate these tumultuous waters the right way—and as soon as we can.

It is difficult when you are in the midst of a storm to try and reinforce the ship in order to survive the storm. It is much easier to prepare your vessel in the harbor for any perils that the sea may throw at you. Yet it seems that so many of us are trying to hear from God and receive help only when the waves of grief begin crashing upon us, and the winds of despair start blowing so loud that trying to hear anything other than our own pain seems impossible. Even still, if you find yourself shipwrecked due to tragedy, and grief is your only companion, there is help for you. There is a hope and a love for you that can pierce through the pain.

I know how painful and devastating grief can be. I have lost my mom, my dad, and many of my uncles and aunts. One of my aunts was tragically, suddenly, and horribly murdered. I have lost cousins. I have even lost my best friend. To my greater dismay, due to the customs and culture of India, where I was born, the bodies of my loved ones had to be buried or cremated within eight hours. I was denied closure and a funeral—something we often take for granted here in the United States.

Even after all that I have experienced, with all of the pain and turmoil that this world and our enemy has thrown at me, I remain steady, peaceful, and full of joy. How? The short answer is very simple: I know my God, and I know His Word. So, I stand as a testimony, and I present the truth of God's Word concerning this somewhat taboo subject of grief. If your heart is heavy with grief, I urge you to read on and find the hope and help for which you've been searching.

If you want to help loved ones who have been suffering with grief, but you don't know what to say, then read on and let God's Word show you how to show your love to them the way He does. In addition, nothing is less threatening to another person than giving them a small, simple book to read. Please use this book to sow a seed of love. Let them pick it up and read it whenever they are ready or as the Lord prompts them.

CHAPTER 1

What Is Grief?

*B*efore we can understand how to walk through our grief, we must first understand what grief is. Grief can seem like a mysterious pain of the heart. Very simply put, grief is an emotion—an emotion that follows loss. The greater the person or thing is to you, the greater your grief will be with the loss.

You can feel grief when you lose an item that held significant sentimental value to you. You can feel grief whenever you see the beautiful house, which you spent years building, go up in flames. You can feel grief when you have worked your entire life to achieve something, and due to an unfortunate accident, injury, or circumstance, that achievement is lost, and your future is unknown. You can spend your life building a family. Then one day you are served divorce papers and you must grieve the loss of your marriage. There are many ways in which we can be touched by this painful and confusing emotion, but there is one predominate type of grief that puts all the others to shame: the grief that follows the death of a loved one.

So, we know that grief is an emotion, but where is the heart trauma originating whenever its effects are reverberating throughout the entirety of our lives?

You are a three-part being. You are a spirit, you have a soul, and you are currently living in a body. Sometimes people get confused and think a soul is some existential entity that does not really exist. The truth is that our spirit has a soul that can feel emotions.

Jesus had a soul, and He felt many emotions while He was living on the earth. He still has a soul, and He still feels emotions. We can get so caught up in the holiness of Christ that we forget that He can feel just as deeply, if not more so, than you and I do. Our Father God and the Holy Spirit are not devoid of feelings and emotions either. Many times, the Bible talks about how certain actions caused emotional responses in our Creator and Father. Just as you can be grieved, so can the Spirit of the Lord be grieved. You are not serving an indifferent, emotionless God.

What Is Grief?

One of the very first things that you must accept when it comes to grief is the simple truth that God loves you. The Bible says that we see through a glass "dimly lit." This means that we do not have the whole picture of things. We only see in part. Many times, when we are stricken with grief, it can cause us to be in so much pain that we begin to lash out at our friends, our family members, and yes—even God. But God loves you, and He feels for you deeply. Grief can make you want to cut everyone out of your life, but please don't cut out the Source of your life. Take all of your pain and confusion to God. You are not alone.

Grief is a condition of the soul. When it comes to processing grief, we must use a combination of the natural and supernatural to navigate our emotions and allow our souls to heal. We do this by applying the truth of God's Word and through the practicality of being prepared, using wisdom, and letting both God and other people help us.

CHAPTER 2

THE STAGES OF GRIEF

I have been in the funeral home with loved ones gathered around, staring death in the face. I have been in a hospital, as well as in many, many emergency rooms, with people beholding horrific sights and realities. It is through these experiences and many like them that I have come to understand the first stage of grief: *shock*.

The second is only a natural response to shock. It happens as husbands are ushering their crying wives out of the rooms. It happens when the sweet, innocent child can't open her eyes to say she loves you. It happens when reality becomes so painful that you can only relate the sensation to a nightmare—one from which you rapidly try to wake up. The second stage of grief is *denial*.

The next stage is a volatile one. Shock is when you have too much emotional input for your body to process. Denial tries to explain, through your mental processing, all that emotional input. Then the third stage tries to release that emotional pressure. You end up exploding into stage three—*anger*—and you begin blaming those around you. You're angry at God. You're angry at other people. You're angry at everybody. Sometimes you don't know why you are angry. You may even end up becoming angry at yourself. People have even become angry at the person who died.

Eventually, as time passes, you realize that regardless of who is to blame, you are still left without your loved one. This realization will hurt you like a dagger in your heart. And if you don't watch out, it will drag you into stage four: *depression*. A dark, black cloud will hang over you, and you won't be able to see the light. You don't see how you can make it without your momma, or your daddy, or your husband, or your wife, or your son, or your daughter, or whomever you have lost. You don't want to see anybody, leave the house, go to work, or do anything at all.

Many people, Christians and non-Christians alike, have become stuck in stage four—or have even been claimed by it. But if you can get through stage four, the fifth and final stage is *acceptance*. Acceptance doesn't mean that your life will ever return to normal. Many times, however, you will discover a new normal and begin to see things differently.

CHAPTER 3

PRACTICALLY PROCESSING GRIEF

When it comes to processing grief, there are many things that help us deal with the different stages we experience, but we also need to know how to handle grief in the long-term. I'm calling these: *keys to help you process your grief.* Unlike the stages of grief, these keys are useful and can be implemented in no particular order. Everyone deals with grief differently, so one key may be especially effective for you, while another may have a minimal impact. However, I believe that all of them will help you manage, process, and move through your grief.

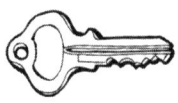 The first key to processing grief is *not to bottle it up.*

Life is a collection of events—the good, the bad, and the ugly. Life is actually energy in motion—and so is grief. Grief has to go *through* you; if you won't let it go through you, you'll end up wrecking your very soul from this bottled-up energy. Don't resist it. Don't deny it or shove it deep inside. And more than ever, please don't bottle it up.

Emotions are very much a part of life. They are a real thing. Even when you have grieved, there will be times when you feel that same grief again, and you'll need to process that emotion, deal with it, let it out, and continue on with life.

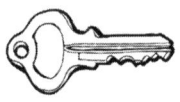 The next key to processing grief is *not to put an expiration date on it.*

Maybe your momma has been gone for one year, and you're still crying. Don't let anybody put an expiration date on your grief or tell you when you should stop grieving your loved one. Grief is an emotion, and you cannot just "fix it" by the power of your will.

Now, on the other hand, this truth doesn't give you a license to let your grief turn into a spirit of grief. A spirit of grief has come upon you when you put everything in your life on hold indefinitely, when you allow your life to just stop. Your hope, your love, and your light all become consumed with heaviness. When you bottle up your grief, and you meditate on it day and night, then you are courting a spirit of grief. This happens far too often in many people's lives.

Remember that grieving is a process. The process can take longer for some people, and it may be shorter for others. Don't focus on how long it took someone else. Because it is a process, you've got to go through it; don't avoid it—keep moving through it! Otherwise, you will get stuck somewhere in the middle of the process and stay there far too long than is good for you. I know people who experienced the death of a loved one twenty years ago, and they are still stuck in their grief. The only way out of grief is to go through it.

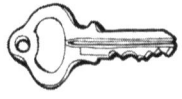 The next key to processing your grief is *to give yourself time.*

The first few months and the first year after losing your loved one will be difficult. It just will be. It has nothing to do with your salvation. I'm talking about your emotions. It will be hard losing your momma, losing your daddy, your son, or your daughter. But don't let grief define who you are during this period. You are still a child of God.

Experiencing grief does not indicate a lack of faith. It is okay to weep whenever a loved one leaves or when you miss them. Many times, Christians can end up being the worst comforters and helpers of those in grief. Even though their loved one is with Jesus now, that person's gain is our loss. Even Paul understood this:

> *For I am in a strait betwixt two, having a desire to depart, and to be with Christ; which is far better: Nevertheless to abide in the flesh is more needful for you.*
>
> —Philippians 1:23–24 kjv

Remember that while you are processing grief, give yourself the time you need, and give others time, as well.

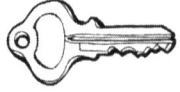

The next key to processing grief is *to talk about the loved one whom you have lost.*

I often talk about the good times I had in the 1970s and 1980s with my mom. Some of the stories I have written about in this book took place when I was preaching with my grandfather in the 1960s, but to me it seems like just yesterday. Though my loved ones may not be here physically, they keep on living in my memories. That's why I always tell this to any family who is hurting and struggling with having lost a loved one: "Sit down and talk." Talk about the good times. Every time you get together, you can tell the same stories, but in different ways. One person may stretch the truth about the loved one to add some humor; somebody else may add some salt and pepper to the story; somebody else might add some cayenne pepper; and somebody else might put in some hot sauce—but it's all the same story! You'll laugh and cry, but you'll also be processing the grief together instead of bottling it up.

Take those memories and pass them along to the next generation. Let your love and admiration and the special moments you shared with your loved ones who have passed live on through your children and grandchildren.

After spending time together, after you return home and start to feel that heaviness come upon you again, take comfort in the fact that you will eventually come out on the other side of the heaviness. Know that you might not be "okay" at first, but that you "will be okay" in the long run.

This sentiment is the next key to processing your grief and consists of a powerful little word: *hope*. The key is *to hold on to your hope.*

Hope is a powerful thing. If there is one thing that will cause you to get stuck right in the middle of a certain stage of grief, it would be the lack or loss of hope. Having hope doesn't mean that you can see your future without your loved one. It doesn't even mean that you can see a path to wholeness. Hope tells you that some way, sometime in the future, you are going to be okay—because you have God on your team.

 The next key to processing your grief is *to understand that it is normal.*

Grief is normal. You should be more concerned about your mental and emotional state if you are *not* grieving when a loved one dies than if you are. Even Jesus, our Lord and Savior, grieved when His friend, Lazarus, died. In John 11:35, the Bible tells us, *"Jesus wept"* (KJV).

Jesus was hurting because Martha and Mary, His good friends, were hurting. The Bible says that Jesus loved Martha, Mary, and Lazarus. And if Jesus cried when Lazarus died, you can be sure that we are going to cry and feel deeply, as well, when someone we love dies.

The next key to processing grief is *to realize that death is unavoidable.*

When we are busy living life and we're healthy and strong, we rarely think about death. Yet, three people die every second; 6,300 people die every hour; and 152,000 people die every day. No one is still walking around the world today who was born in the seventeenth century. Yet, in some way or another, most of us have convinced ourselves that we will wake up, go through our daily routines, go to bed at the end of the day, and continue doing that forever. This is not our reality. As the Bible says:

> *And as it is appointed unto men once to die, but after this the judgment.*
>
> —Hebrews 9:27 kjv

All of us will die if the Lord doesn't rapture us beforehand. We do not need to meditate constantly on our mortality, but it should be taken into consideration when we deal with others, when we plan for the future, and as we work to make the most out of every day that we have been given on the earth. Do not make your grieving process harder than it has to be by not spending time with your loved ones while you can or not sharing with them just how much they mean to you while you can.

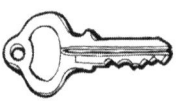

The next key to processing our grief is *to realize the brevity of life.*

Job experienced grief very heavily, so much so that God paid him a visit while he was in his grief-stricken state. If anyone could speak to us about losing a loved one or about how to deal with grief, it would be Job. He said: "It is God who decides when my time is" (see Job 14), and he compared our lives to a flower, a shadow, and even the grass. He eventually reconciled his fear of death and began to trust his life to God. He also realized, after witnessing death and experiencing the immeasurable grief that followed it, that life is short.

I have conducted many funerals, but the hardest one had a tiny casket at the front of the church with a four-month preemie baby inside. I also conducted the funeral of a 105-year-old mother—the matriarch of her family. The book of Job taught me that in both cases—whether you are a four-month-old preemie infant or a 105-year-old grandmother, compared to eternity, each of our lives is short.

That's why David said this: *"Lord, remind me how brief my time on earth will be. Remind me that my days are numbered—how fleeting my life is"* (Psalm 39:4 NLT). This truth is important for us to understand so that we can continue to live our lives in the wake of tragedy. It may be tough to pull yourself out of bed in the morning, and it may seem as if there is nothing still keeping you on this earth, but your days are already short; it won't be long until you are with your loved ones in heaven. While you are still here on the earth, you are meant to fight. Fight for Christ. Fight to finish your race. Fight to love even when all you feel is despair. Since your days are already numbered, don't spend them all stuck in the middle of the grief process. Move through the process and get to the other side.

CHAPTER 4

BE PREPARED!

*H*aving been a pastor since 1994 and having been in full-time ministry for forty-one years, I've dealt with many "natural" details that accompany the passing of a loved one. There are certain practical things we can do that will help our loved ones to deal with their grief at our passing.

Some Christians seem to think that discussing any preparations for their passing with their family members is somehow demonstrating a lack of faith—as if admitting that you will one day die shows a lack of faith. That is a rather silly notion, because if the Lord doesn't come back in the next one hundred years, there won't be one person left alive from your generation by that time. Remember, there is not one person still walking around who was born in the 1700s. We should prepare for the day when we or our loved ones pass on—not just spiritually, but practically, as well.

Here are some practical things you can do today to prepare for the passing of you or your family members.

First, *consider getting life and/or burial insurance.* If you can't afford it currently, that's okay. However, you should eventually get something that ensures that whenever you pass, your death will not burden the loved ones you leave behind.

Second, *decide with your family whether you want to be buried, be cremated, or donate your body to medical science.* After you are gone, they will be dealing with their pain and grief, and having to make decisions about your body on top of that can be overwhelming. So, make the decision for them and let them know your wishes before anything happens to you.

In addition, *communicate to your loved ones about what kind of memorial service you want:* what songs you want to have played at your funeral, who you want to have speak, and so on. This will help your loved ones when you go home to be with the Lord. And the same applies for your loved ones sharing their wishes with you. These small preparations can make things so much easier for those left behind in their time of grief.

Finally, please *draw up a will for yourself,* and be sure your loved ones have taken this step as well. Make sure it is a legally binding will so that there will be no question about the decedent's wishes. If, for whatever reason, you don't want to draw up a will, then take whatever God has blessed you with, and do me a favor: Get with your family members and give them what you plan to give them while you're still alive. That way they won't kill each other and have to plan another family funeral!

Because I have been a pastor for more than forty years, I have been around grief and have conducted many funerals. I assure you, taking these practical steps before your own passing or that of your loved ones will help you and promote peace among your family members.

CHAPTER 5

WE DO NOT GRIEVE AS THE WORLD GRIEVES

*A*s we have seen, death is the separation of the spirit and soul from the body. The body stays here on the earth and decays, but the spirit and the soul live forever.

As Christians, we must look at our lives from heaven's viewpoint. Realize that the Christian loved one who died has gained heaven, rather than focusing on your loss here on earth. Sometimes we get so selfish about what we want. We just think about us, us, us. The book of Psalms tells us that the homegoing of God's children is precious in His sight (see Psalm 116:15). Your loved ones who have passed on have actually gone home. They are excited, and all of heaven is excited!

Paul wrote in the book of Romans, *"We don't live for ourselves or die for ourselves. If we live, it's to honor the Lord. And if we die, it's to honor the Lord."* Then he concludes, *"So whether we live or die, we belong to the Lord"* (14:7–8 NLT). When we die, we are still His—and we are going home to be with Him forever. You need to think of it from the viewpoint of your loved one. Paul wrote in the book of Philippians, *"For to me to live is Christ, and to die is gain"* (1:21 KJV). That is an amazing statement that runs contrary to our usual way of thinking. Paul was saying that it is better for us to die and go to heaven than to continue living in this fallen world. Your loved one who has passed away has not lost anything; instead, they have gained everything—heaven itself.

On February 7, 2021, I was talking to my wife and my children, and I suddenly realized that if my mom had still been alive, she would have turned one hundred years old on that very day. Many of us are sad when a loved one's birthday comes around after they have passed away. But guess what? They have a birthday every day in heaven! I now look at my mother's passing from *her* viewpoint. She's not suffering anymore, thank God! She has joined the great cloud of witnesses (see Hebrews 12:1).

Heaven is a real place. That may sound obvious, but sometimes one of the best things you can do, right there in the middle of your grief-stricken state, is to picture your loved one smiling, pain-free, dancing, rejoicing, laughing, and having a wonderful time up in heaven with Jesus and all your other family members and loved ones.

In John 14:1–6, Jesus said in a matter of words: "I go to prepare a place for you. I'm coming back. I'm going to take you with Me back home to heaven." Do you know why He said these words? Because they are true! God wants to be with you more than you could ever want to be with God. When I'm here living on the earth, God is with me. But when I die, I'm still with Him—in heaven.

The last time I saw my mom was in January 1982. How did I deal with her loss in my life? I knew that I will see her again. I have an *assurance* that I will see her again. I *believe* I'm going to see my mom, my dad, even my grandfather, who prayed for me when he was alive. I'm going to see all of them, and when I do, we will never have to be apart from each other again. We will be there forever and ever, and that brings me so much comfort. It gives me a comfort that the world cannot understand, because death for them is final. For believers, death has been defanged—and it has lost its sting. Praise the Lord!

CHAPTER 6

YOU ARE NOT ALONE

*A*bove all, remember that God is with you. I've been there, and I know what it's like when your physical strength doesn't amount to anything. I've been there, and I know what it's like to hear the earth-shattering news of a loved one's passing. I've been there, and I know what it's like to tremble all night with grief. I've been through times when I couldn't even hold a glass of water steady enough to drink it because of my emotional state, and I am a pastor—I'm strong in the Lord! Well, this "strong pastor" needed his wife's help even to get a drink of water. Yet, even in the midst of my grief-stricken state, I was *never without hope.* I never came to the conclusion that my life was over. I knew that "this, too, shall pass." Even on my darkest days, I *always* had hope. That hope was bread to my soul because of the revelation that God loved me, would help me, and would never leave me to face my grief alone.

A common phrase that I hear at funerals is this: "Once we get to heaven, God will wipe away all your tears." Although that statement is very true, we don't have to wait until heaven for Him to wipe our tears away! I'm a witness. God has done it for me—in this life! God will wipe away your tears, too—now, in this life. He will help you deal with all of your sorrows and your grief. Remember, *He is One who is acquainted with grief.* God will stay with you as long as you let Him, because He is your Father!

That is the truth: You have a Father. Whether or not you have an earthly father who has your back, you always have a heavenly Father who is watching out for you. The Bible tells us that when we became Christians, we were adopted into the family of God. Too many believers have looked at God as their boss, their Lord, the One they must obey, but they seem to forget that He is actually their *Father*. Christ and His work on the cross turned us from slaves into sons:

> *You didn't receive a spirit of slavery to lead you back again into fear, but you received a Spirit that shows you*

are adopted as his children. With this Spirit, we cry, "Abba, Father."

—Romans 8:15 CEB

Don't be afraid to run to your Father with your emotions. Grief can be a fickle thing, and it can cause many of us to run from the very One whom we desperately need the most. The comfort you are looking for is found in Him. Paul's words in 2 Corinthians tell us this:

Blessed be the God and Father of our Lord Jesus Christ, the Father of mercies and God of all comfort.

—2 Corinthians 1:3 NKJV

Did you catch that? Our God is the God of *all* comfort. My absolute favorite verse that speaks to how much God is moved by our grief is found in the book of Isaiah:

> *"The Spirit of the Lord God is upon Me, because the Lord has anointed Me to preach good tidings to the poor; He has sent Me to heal the brokenhearted, to proclaim liberty to the captives, and the opening of the prison to those who are bound; to proclaim the acceptable year of the Lord, and the day of vengeance of our God; to comfort all who mourn, to console those who mourn in Zion, to give them beauty for ashes, the oil*

of joy for mourning, the garment of praise for the spirit of heaviness; that they may be called trees of righteousness, the planting of the LORD, that He may be glorified."

—Isaiah 61:1–3 NKJV

Grief can make you feel like a captive in your own body. It can make you feel bound up, held hostage, and helpless to escape. Grief can cause you to weep until there are no more tears left to shed. A broken heart is one filled with grief. And if left unchecked, grief can turn into the spirit of heaviness. Yet God loves you so much that He sent Jesus, and He has come to exchange your broken heart for His healing touch. He wants to trade your bondage and captivity for His freedom. He longs to swap your ashes for His beauty and your mourning for His joy!

The reason the word *ashes* is used in this Scripture passage is because back in the day, when people mourned the loss of a loved one or family member, they would pour ashes over their heads and then sit in their grief and sorrow.

This one truth has gotten me through so many things, including my own times of mourning: God is your Father, and *you are never alone.* Your momma, your daddy, your spouse, your child, your loved ones—they *all* may have passed away, but God is still there for you! Your relationship with Him will never end. Even when your earthly body perishes, your relationship with God will transcend this life and continue into the next.

These two Scripture verses are beautiful reminders that even when it seems like we have been left all alone in this world, there is One who will never, ever leave us:

> *Yea, though I walk through the valley of the shadow of death, I will fear no evil; for You are with me; Your rod and Your staff, they comfort me.*
>
> —PSALM 23:4 NKJV

For He has said, "I will never [under any circumstances] desert you [nor give you up nor leave you without support, nor will I in any degree leave you helpless], nor will I forsake or let you down or relax My hold on you [assuredly not]!"

—Hebrews 13:5 AMP

If His Word was the only help you had, that would be enough—but your heavenly Father didn't stop there. He sent Jesus!

Grief can be so potent that it makes you feel as if you were the only one in the entire world who is experiencing this amount of pain. The truth is, there are many others out there who have experienced what you are going through. Some people have gone through it, some people are going through it right now, and some people have been completely defeated by it. When it comes to processing grief, talking about what you are going through is paramount to your recovery. One of the worst things that you can do is bottle up everything you are feeling. This will cause so much pain and suffering for you, until you eventually explode in the worst way possible. Who is the one you can open up to, the person with whom you can talk about your pain? Sometimes it may feel like you are dumping all of your baggage on someone else when you talk about your problems. And the chances of there being somebody close to you who has gone through what you are currently going through is rare. So, what are we to do? Certainly, there is wisdom in leaning on your pastor, friends, or a godly counselor. Never be afraid to reach out for help. However, even if it seems like there is nobody on earth who understands what you are going through and just how deep your pain is, remember: There is One who knows exactly what you are going through. His name is Jesus. The Bible tells us this in the book of Isaiah:

> ***He is despised and rejected by men, a Man of sorrows and acquainted with***

grief. And we hid, as it were, our faces from Him; He was despised, and we did not esteem Him.

—Isaiah 53:3 NKJV

Jesus was called a "man of sorrows." We don't often picture Jesus as having dealt with any sorrows when He was here on the earth, but the Bible not only reveals that He dealt with His fair share of grief—so much so that He was identified by His sorrows by the prophet—but the Scripture also takes it a step further: *He was "acquainted with grief."*

Friend, Jesus is all too acquainted with the grief you are experiencing. He has seen millions of His brothers and sisters reject the gifts that He died to give them. He walked this earth as we do—and not even Jesus was immune to grief. Therefore, do not for a moment think that you have done something wrong, or that you haven't had enough faith, because you are experiencing grief. Even the Man who never sinned could not avoid being "acquainted with grief." Therefore, don't condemn yourself for experiencing grief.

Jesus knew grief even deeper than our own. Not only did He experience all of the physical pain that came along with the cross, He also experienced the sheer emotional and spiritual turmoil of God turning His back on Him—a deep level of grief that those of us who call God Father will never know.

Jesus is always and forever your friend and ally. You don't have to search desperately for someone to talk to who understands your situation, who knows how you feel, and who has the answers you are looking for. *Jesus* fits that description—and He is always available to you. The Bible speaks to this truth in the book of Hebrews:

> ***Inasmuch then as we [believers] have a great High Priest who has [already ascended and] passed through the heavens, Jesus the Son of God, let us hold fast our confession [of faith and cling tenaciously to our absolute***

trust in Him as Savior]. For we do not have a High Priest who is unable to sympathize and understand our weaknesses and temptations, but One who has been tempted [knowing exactly how it feels to be human] in every respect as we are, yet without [committing any] sin. Therefore let us [with privilege] approach the throne of grace [that is, the throne of God's gracious favor] with confidence and without fear, so that we may receive mercy [for our failures] and find [His amazing] grace to help in time of need [an appropriate blessing, coming just at the right moment].

—Hebrews 4:14–16 AMP

Jesus understands and sympathizes with what you are going through. You can approach God, your Father, and Jesus, your Brother, with boldness to obtain the help you are seeking. He will always bring well-timed help to you, help that comes just when we need it!

Finally, my friend, God saw fit not only to send Jesus, and not only to adopt you into His family, but also to send you His very own Spirit to reside within you every moment of every day. The same Spirit that raised Christ from the dead lives in you! He is not just a stowaway, either. Christ said this about the Holy Spirit: *"And I will ask the Father, and He will give you another Helper (Comforter, Advocate, Intercessor—Counselor, Strengthener, Standby), to be with you forever"* (John 14:16 AMP).

We have *another* Comforter. In other words, we already had one comforter: The disciples to whom Jesus was speaking already had Him to comfort them—as do we. But God sent us another Comforter so that we never have to go searching to find our help, our comfort, our advocate, our strength, or our counsel. All we have to do now is to lift our voices right in the middle of our mess and call out to the Holy Spirit for help!

The Holy Spirit is our Comforter. Whenever things do not work out the way we plan, He is there to love us and care for us. When we feel alone, He is there to let us know that we are never truly alone.

> *Then had the churches rest throughout all Judaea and Galilee and Samaria, and were edified; and walking in the fear of the Lord, and <u>in the comfort of the Holy Ghost</u>, were multiplied.*
>
> —Acts 9:31 kjv, emphasis mine

Even when you feel confused, hurt, and broken, you can speak to the Holy Spirit right in the middle of your circumstances, and the Holy Spirit will speak through you and to you in return. You may be so heartbroken that you don't even know what to pray. That is okay, too! You don't *have* to know how to pray. You can just lift your voice and speak in tongues as the Holy Spirit gives you utterance, and you will pray the perfect prayer! God knows exactly what you need. You have your heavenly Father, you have Jesus, and you have the Holy Spirit—all ready and willing to help you. Truly, since God did not withhold even one of these most precious things from us, don't you think we should trust Him even when we don't understand? Shouldn't we move forward, process our grief, and quit blaming God and others? Your loved one may have meant everything to you, but you mean everything to God. Trust God—He is with you!

ABOUT THE AUTHOR

Born and reared in the nation of India, Pastor Stephen Rathod graduated from high school at the age of sixteen in Ahmedabad, Gujarat, India. He entered Gujarat University in 1966 and graduated in 1970 with a Bachelor of Science Degree in Chemistry. In June 1974, he received his Master's Degree in Organic Chemistry from the same university. Afterward, he came to the United States to further his education. In May 1977, he received a Bachelor of Science in Petroleum Engineering from the University of Tulsa, Oklahoma.

In September 1974, he answered the call of God to serve Him in full-time ministry. He entered Rhema Bible Training Center in the fall of 1977 and received a Diploma for Ministerial Training on May 19, 1978. In August 1980, he was ordained as a pastor by the founder of Redeemed Christian Church of God, the late Reverend Josiah Akiundayomi, in Lagos, Nigeria. In January 1982, Pastor Rathod was ordained through Faith Christian Fellowship International Church Inc. under the leadership of Dr. and Mrs. Doyle "Buddy" Harrison. In June 1990, he received a Master's of Theological

Studies from Logos Bible College and Graduate School. From this same school, he received a Doctor of Ministry in 1992 and a Doctor of Philosophy (Missiology) in August 1996.

Since 1979, Pastor Rathod has done extensive missionary work in Africa (Nigeria and Botswana), Burma, India, Philippines, England, and throughout the United States. In India, he and his brother established a ministry called CRY (Christ Reconciling Youth to God) Ministries in Gujarat State. He also ministers at the Tulsa County Detention Center and on the streets of Tulsa.

Pastor Rathod has been an active member of Covenant Family Church since 1980. He became its Senior Pastor in September 1994. Stephen and his wife, Lee, reside in Tulsa, Oklahoma.

To contact Pastor Stephen Rathod:
Covenant Family Church
725 East 36 Street North
Tulsa, OK 74106
918-428-3875

covenantfc@tulsacoxmail.com

https://www.covenantfamilychurchtulsa.com

You can find his messages on YouTube channel Covenant Family Church Tulsa.